Figs
&
Falling

Written and Illustrated
by
Sierra Selwa Aldulaimi

Published by Sierra Selwa Aldulaimi
© 2024 Sierra Selwa Aldulaimi

ISBN: 979-8-9913464-0-5
Library of Congress Control Number: 2024916933

Illustrations and Cover by Sierra Selwa Aldulaimi

Sierra Selwa Aldulaimi
Calimesa, California, United States of America
Website: sierraselwa.com

Preface

The following pages are an honest reckoning with existence. I hope you find connection here.

Grief doesn't always look like you'd expect.
She is an angsty teenager, finding her place in the world
Not always wearing black clothes of mourning - sometimes
it IS just a phase.
Maybe today she'll throw on a flowing dress and watch its
subtle dance in the wild.
You may not recognize her, but it is still the same grief
The grief you watched be born on a dark day in a hospital.

Grief does not fade away, but grows into a woman
Occasionally overshadowed by her friends
heartache and joy and exhaustion and adventure
Yes, joy and grief are friends.
They've known each other since the beginning, though you
did not see them together
Remember - grief does not always look like you'd expect.
For grief can laugh and joy can cry
And she is not birthed out of death alone
But she is formed when something has been lost
Loss of relationship
of sense of self
of home
of freedom
of a life
of security
of everything you once knew

Now, you may look at her and see prison without parole, or
an inescapable, scary forest
But that is not her.
Get to know her
Look her in the eyes and grab her by the hand
Let her show you nostalgia
Allow her to walk you through growth
May she introduce you to hope.

Medium - May 6, 2019

A new medium

Not a new middle,

      Though that does sound intriguing.

A different way to create

A medium

Maybe today I will paint on different colored paper

      Hoping to produce something out of my ordinary.

I suppose calling it a middle isn't that off.

The paper in the middle of my hand and the painted vision,

The poem in the middle of me and my truth.

It is neither good,

      nor bad,

Simply medium

Chill Hits Playlist on Spotify - May 7, 2019

What did they put in this song?

It seems to be sweetened with nostalgia and a heavy bass line.

Or maybe it is laced with intoxicating mystery and synth.

No way could these strings be directionless, unintentional.

Could they possibly conceptualize the impact this melody has on my soul?

The muscles in my body disappear for a moment,

While a riff takes control

I am the song now.

Laced with mystery and synth.

Morse Code - May 10, 2019

I awoke into an artist's haven

The water falling in morse code

      its messages full of angst, but still speaking in cliches

"Nothing matters and no one understands,

now stay in bed or come out and dance."

I know from elementary that the clouds are weighing heavy

I feel it in my bones and from what it asks of me -

Now's your chance

      to feel your sad

           to sulk in gloom

                to speak in metaphors and be pretentiously profound.

The Safest Place I've Known - May 16, 2019

I spend every day with my body.
I thought I knew her like, well, the back of my hand.
Like the best friend that I spend hours at coffee with,
divulging secrets we wouldn't dare share with anyone else.
A fair assumption since we are always together.
But she is more like the person who rides the same train as
you to work everyday.
You're familiar with one another, but there is no true
exchange.
Or the waiter at your favorite restaurant. Light banter on a
regular basis, but no depth. You don't even know their last
name.
I took advantage of having her around all the time, never
taking a moment to listen to her.

But I am lucky, because she was patient.
She waited for me.
And though I did not listen to her, she heard me.
She knew me.
She waited for me when I did things to hurt her.
She tried to warn me when I was being unkind to myself.
I thought she was deadweight, in the way of my fast-paced
ambition.
She did what she could to slow me down, because she knew
I was exhausted.
She waited for me.

Until she couldn't anymore.
She pulled me by my guts, and held my shaking hands.
And she cleared her throat and decided to speak a little
louder.
Though her voice was hoarse and unfamiliar, it still felt just
like home.
Flashbacks came from times she'd spoken, and I'd called her
by wrong names.
Maybe fate, or god above, or forces that are unknown.

But she was with me all along.
She'd gotten me here.

Little did I know, she has so much good to say.
I try to listen more and more.
And when she is too tired to speak any longer,
I will wait for her.

Hodgepodge - June 9, 2019

I've been liking myself lately. Seems silly to say. Both in the way that it is so simple, but also so fleeting.
I like myself today.
But I will wake up in the morning with the kind of zit that makes me wish I had an entirely new face. Or I will walk up a long flight of stairs and feel so out of breath that I will loathe myself for not exercising enough. Or decide that the freckles on my skin, that I quite like today, are too dark or too light or too many or not enough.
I do not know what it will be or when it will hit. Tomorrow or a month from now.
I will decide that embodiment is not for me. That my redeeming qualities are not redemptive enough. I am sure of it. It has happened so often before. Sometimes for a few hours after a bad look in the mirror. Or for months on end, wondering if I will ever like the bony structure of my nose
the course texture of my hair
the wrinkles that have appeared far too early
the length of my fingers
the ambiguity of my eye color

And then I do.
Like today, when I step back and see how all of those features play with each other
The interaction amongst those quirks and the light in my eye and the beaming of my smile when I decide
it's all okay with me

record player - June 10, 2019

you are warmth
the safest kind like waking on a winter day
wrapped up in blankets full of body heat
you are a productive day
the sort that makes you close your eyes
knowing that things are going the way you hoped
you are a song
that I cannot decide whether to only listen in headphones
and keep, so intimately, to myself
or to play on speakers at full volume
and share with the world
you deserve to be heard

Tag - June 10, 2019

I want to be good. And I want to be right. And I am so scared. So scared of getting caught. If I write and I'm a fraud and they will know and they will… they will… They will do something and I assume it will be bad. Or they will do nothing, I suppose. They may not care. And maybe that's worse but is no reason to be scared.

I am playing tag and I am so petrified of being caught that I hide up a tree. I was so scared and I fled. But there is nothing to do up in this tree. No one even knows I'm gone. I just watch. And someone screams. They've been tagged. But they still smile. Somehow being 'it' is not all that bad. And they run and they run. It may just be fun to be tagged. But I am in the clouds, not being missed. And for once I wish to be out of breath.

Tipping the Scale - June 12, 2019

An asteroid hit my planet
I went on like nothing was wrong
I remained in perfect motion
Despite death and damage, ruins
All there was to do was spin
Keep on orbiting the sun,
who could not see the massive rock
that wreaked havoc on my life
but it was fine
and hurt
but fine
Until a pebble hit my planet
so small, so unassuming
And I could not stay in motion
Was it the added weight -
too much, on top of what the astroid brought?
Or a reminder of the trauma done by rocks,
to me, before?

Abundance - June 13, 2019

I have lived these twenty years only knowing scarcity
I could not leave your house without milking every minute
we could spare
Kissing you too many times
Only driven by the fear
Not enough time to spend together
Not enough days to press my body safely into yours
All of my favorite days ended with panic
How do I stay in this moment forever?

Perhaps the fear fueled by scarcity sets in
When you see the brevity of life before your eyes
When you lose something(someone) forever
Or maybe its always been there
I cannot know when it began
It's all that I remember

Then you introduced me to abundance

You felt the desperation every time I told you goodbye
My anxious coping
And you introduced me to abundance
Kissing you only out of sheer bliss
No motivation of fear
I left the beach with you today
A perfect day
With no regard for scarcity
You give me so much life

A Letter to My Fan - June 14, 2019

I am learning to love you. I have spent so long thinking that you were my enemy. Holding me back from living. Plagued by anxiety. Or overwhelmed by exhaustion. You do not always look the way that I hope. You are unpredictable. At least that is what I thought, because I never took time to get to know you. If I had, I would have seen all that you do to take care of me. All of the ways you try to protect me. Those inconveniences, the ways you seemed like a burden were your efforts to tell me something was wrong. I'm sorry I took so long to listen. You have brought me through so much. I owe you everything. I will do my best to take care of you. I will dress you up in fun things. I will take you to yoga. I will let you rest. But mostly, I will listen to you. And I will speak more kindly to you. And tell you I love you. And tell the world I love you. Thank you, body, for getting me here.

All of a Sudden I Love To Do Chores - July 6, 2019

I wake up and I take so long getting out of bed / I get ready so slowly / I empty the dishwasher / Start the laundry / Spend far too long on Youtube / Reorganize my room / I do all the chores that I usually hate / I do anything else except what I really need to do / What at my core, I really want to do / I fill my days with every possible task except creating / I place my fingers on anything I can find except those piano keys / I write instagram captions and compose long texts to friends / I write anything except songs / I tell myself I am too busy / I tell myself I am too tired / I find every excuse / Every escape / Except the truth that I have no idea what I am doing

Santa Barbara - July 12, 2019

we are back from our little trip, just the two of us. a getaway
- so serene, so surreal. i was, and still am, overtaken by the
simple happiness that i felt just being with you. still i kept
coming back to the thought, "i hope this memory stays good
forever" and "please god let nothing ever taint this beautiful
moment in my life." i know i am young. and i learned while
even younger that nothing lasts. it is life's greatest promise
and curse. so while i am not so naive to ask for that perfect
moment to last forever, i was still asking for something to
last. for the good memory to last. for these few days to
remain sacred. i am not asking for a loaf of bread to stay
fresh forever. i know the effects of the elements are
inevitable, be it mold or dryness. i am holding on to hope
that i will remember what that bread tasted like for a long
time. that i will keep thinking about its texture, its softness,
and know that it was so damn good.

November and December - July 13, 2019

Remember those months before we said 'I love you.'
Our feelings ran like electricity through our bodies.
But we exchanged them with such a tenderness - a caution.
I loved you before those three words were proclaimed.
I cut that love down into small bites.
Much easier to digest.
> *You make me so happy*
> *I want to spend all my time with you*
> *Your skin is soft*
> *You are everything good in the world*

And every trope under the sun
Somehow all feeling less intense
So as not to scare each other away with sparks
Doe-eyed deer
Finally deciding that the currents between us were too much
to be described by anything less vulnerable

String Theory - September 15, 2019

Grief is like a fiber,
Pulled from a thread
Appearing simple and easy to understand
Yet with unique tears
That severed itself from what once was whole
And is composed of much more than what meets the eye
A fiber composed of molecules, and atoms down from there
Not so easily counted
Not so simple to be known
But even if those atoms were accounted for
Enumerated as best can be,
The quantity still does not define all within the fiber
Still those atoms are composed of particles, and those also of particles, and likely more unknowns
That broken part of thread is never so easily understood

Crystal Ball - January 15, 2020

Sometimes I wonder if I've always known
That he'd go before I was grown
Intuition, a prophecy, or a common misstep
A cause and effect
A smoke and then death

A little girl, so many tears
Dad loved cigarettes
She needed him here

UnStuck - March 19, 2020

For all of you who feel stuck,

pulling and prodding and fighting

to get out, to move on, to move up

It's okay
to be still
to let life happen
to observe

Your inaction can be productive

Maybe all you need to get out from under the rubble
Is time

Inhabited - March 31, 2020

Fig trees and orange groves
In the stories we recount
You live in it all

Tired Phrases - April 7, 2020

All I have is ordinary sadness
I do not know where some people find
Such special phrases
Romanticize the mundane
All I have are dictionary words
My universal experiences so tired
My uniqueness too obscure
How do I make my heartache beautiful
Is it worth it
Even I do not find it interesting enough to consume

I cry pain and I spit pain and I write pain and pity
Plain

Final Question - April 13, 2020

He asked your favorite color
And you hazily explained
A beautiful blue
A teal hue
Like that shirt you wore and mom adored

Then that ocean carried you away

HBD - April 22, 2020

Thank you, Earth, for your generosity
May we only take what we need
For your serenity
May we sit in your gentleness
And for your intricacies
May we slow enough to see

Spring Cleaning - April 30, 2020

Softly gazing at tree tops
I curate a space
Rid of distraction
Rid of mess
Rid of unnecessary noise
I strip the "ugly"
I do things "right"
And then it is empty

And there is not much to write about nothing
So little of note in the sterile

Let the mess
There is something to be said about a place that is lived in

Non-exhaustive - June 21, 2020

Things that remind me of you:
To-go cups of Pepsi
Carbs
Grocery stores
Trains
Parents dropping kids off at the high school
Wisdom teeth
Fruit trees

Pieces of you I find in myself:
The thrill of making someone laugh
Beautiful bone structure
A listening ear
Worry
Soft spot for "junk" food
The need to sing loudly (mine hopefully more in tune)

Insomnia - September 20, 2020

12:16am in bed and all I can hear
Is my heartbeat and
The artificial rain sounds from my phone that are
Supposed to drown out the thoughts
Of you being gone
My heart has kept up its beating for years now
It hasn't stopped but yours did.
And now I am left to figure out what to do
With all the heartbeats I have left

I don't know the count
Too many feels lonely
Too few seems unfair

This heart has beaten quite a lot now since you left. And still
I can't sleep
Because I'm dreaming that you're not gone
after all

Do Nothing - September 27, 2020

There is a forbidden beauty in the decision to do nothing. Masked and diminished by the lifeblood of a productivity-based society, you must push past the guilt and shame of the things that appear lazy. But in the middle of a Sunday afternoon when there are dishes to be washed or projects to be completed, you can lay on the couch. And you resist the urge to feel bad, because that is not doing nothing. That is wallowing. You just lay on the couch. Stare at the ceiling (likely the least beautiful or enamoring part of your home). Maybe it feels like a waste of time. Or, there is a chance that the light from the window reflects off of your eyelashes. Now your view of the ceiling is bordered by the natural glittering of light particles on the little hairs that surround your eyes. It is so simple, nearly nothing. You just feel like a person. You are a person existing in the beautiful and the normal.

Listener - October 8, 2020

She sits while I paint a picture of what's in my mind
Made of jumbled up words, so unrefined
She does not seem to be put off by the mess
Or that perhaps I am wasting her time
Desperate for an image emblematic of my
pain. The nodding of your head
Telling me you feel my art.

Thank you for your patience, for your patronage

What I imagine a mother feels like (but it's about a friend)
- October 13, 2020

If I am the nest you had to fly from
at least I felt like home
If I was the hometown you got out of
at least I was your constant
If I was the pacifier you outgrew
at least I was your comfort
Couldn't make you stay
Stay young, stay home, stay safe
But I helped make you

The Eraser - October 24, 2020

You'd think that watching your life flash before your eyes
Means you could recount your life moment by moment
That after the tragedy you would hold close every memory
you've ever made
And yet it seems to act like a faulty reset button
Accidentally, or maybe fully intentionally, clearing out so
many years of experiences and feelings and memories
It's as if any moment where it seems the world is ending,
you lose pieces of your past.
A price you pay for those heavy emotions
You must lay down those conversations in the car, the
birthday parties, and bedtime stories
To carry grief and suffering and shame and sorrow.

Carry-on - November 1, 2020

My bag is too heavy
I have filled it with trash
Empty it, you say
such a simple solution
I'm so used to the weight
of those wrappers, they are expectations
I place upon
myself. And I shame
myself for the strain on my body
Dispose of things piece
by piece
Only to have them replaced
an ugly cycle
I'll start looking
for a new bag, a fresh start

Maternal Instinct - November 2, 2020

There are creations within me
Awaiting birth
  songs and thoughts and poems and dreams
There is no life waiting to be born
No life beyond my own
Albeit selfish or fearful
I am not done being born

Year 7 - March 7, 2021

I tried to condense the loss of you
carried like ashes around my neck
subtle, understated
with me but not of me

but this is not
an accessory to lay on the nightstand

my grief grows in untamable vines
climbing up toward sunlit memories of you

and they stretch out
to others and we are entangled
because we knew you
our missing of you
reaches across waters
to the town that birthed you
and up to the skies that watched over you

echoes travel among the stars
of the beat from my chest
more resonant now
from the hollow place you left

your absence takes up space

your absence takes up   space

Can You Hear Me? - March 31, 2021

there is so much to say
so much to tell you

but there are words that need protecting
memories to be kept sacred

once shared, these thoughts are yours
to do what you please with
ignore or misconstrue
add too much meaning or none at all

so I hold all my words in a motherly embrace
overly protective

Looking for Me and Finding You - April 1, 2021

Roll the car window down
Airing out the stale thoughts
Of self loathing and spiraling
I am caught by the smell of orange blossoms
I thought I missed them this year
Confused on whether they come
in March or April
Inhale over and over
And over again
Lightheaded because I can't seem to get enough
Of this floral magic
I wonder if the people driving
with their windows up
know what they're missing out on
I let my hair frizz out
And I listen to old pop songs
And I feel free and hopeful
My heart still broken
Because the first year that I noticed this
beautiful scent was the year you left
You, who always stole oranges from these same groves
And suddenly I realize that these blossoms smell like magic
and your memory

Scapegoat - April 10, 2021

Is it okay if I blame you
Would you mind taking responsibility

for my shortcomings
for my inability to conform to what is expected

if I never walk down the aisle
because I don't dare to go alone

I know it's not your fault
but since you're not here
can you help what i cannot

On the Run - April 20, 2021

I'll stay busy forever
So I have something to blame
For why
I don't text my friends
Don't see my mom
Don't write songs
It's not my fault
I don't have the time
No time for you on my mind

Would Could Should - May 4, 2021

I wish I would have danced.
There are so many regrets I could have
that I *do* have
To have asked you more questions
about your boyhood
and your dreams and your fears
To have shared conversation in your mother tongue

It's possible I would have missed a step
Let the memory of your stories slip my mind
Allow my californian speech to muddle your first language

I wish I could have been brave
At your side
As your hands raised,
Shoulders shimmied, spirits lifted

But I have no choice but to accept my sideline point of view

HEARTACHE

INCARNATE

Working Overtime - May 8, 2021

My dreams are a meeting place.

It is while I'm asleep that I see my old friends.
Unconsciously, I inquire
was my friendship too much to bear
did you decide I wasn't worth your time
gradually or all at once?

I finally have a chance to confront my exes
The scars of my heart flare
I see anger I did not know
was there

And when I'm painfully lucky
Dad comes to see me
like the child I was when he left,
we play make believe
what life would be

My dreams are settling scores
My dreams are both unapologetic and overly sorry
My dreams are closure
My dreams are peace
My dreams are heartache incarnate

Port Angeles - May 25, 2021

slip your fingers through
the rips in my jeans

you stand in the waves
and watch the world turn
oh free boy, please
stay with me

if you run
can I come
will you slow your pace
so I can keep up

Yours, Mine, and Ours - July 2021

I love finding meaning in cliches
Catching myself in a moment that feels
so magical
I must share its intricacies with anyone who will listen
And yet
They are merely
Falling in love
And watching life work out
Taking a candlelit bath with a good book
The simplicity
The commonplace activity
Is a connection with all those
Who have come before and
Felt such such real human emotion
It is all the same
Still this moment is all mine
My own personal cliche all for me

Just Checking In - Sept 7, 2021

Please ask me how I'm doing and don't wait for my
response. Ask me how I'm doing and answer for me. Be
curious about me. Show me you care. But not too curious or
too caring. Invite me over and then lock me out before I bare
my soul and give you too much.

To Be Loved - Sept 15, 2021

you expect no reintroduction
welcoming my newness
when i flow, you flow

thank you for seeing my today
my now
my self
no yesterdays held against me

my minimalist phase came at a horrible time - Oct 4, 2021

I wonder what was in your closet
what I turned down in my grief riddled haze
the flannels I could be wrapped up in
as I sit in my lonely apartment
wondering what advice you'd offer to me now
relics of the past could only comfort me

it is all gone

and I can only hope that those sick 90s windbreakers
or dorky dad jeans are living on again
with someone who needed
to be clothed with the confidence only you had
if only I knew why I gave up more than I was forced to lose
and if I could go back I'd hoard boxes of old polos
that would never fit me right
because they were yours

not much is anymore
and that is the issue with everything and existing without
you

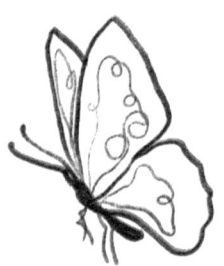

If You Need a Friend - January, 1 2022

We are the only two
Left in this town
And yet one of us
Is in the ground
And though I'm sure
You aren't bound
To that plot of land
If you are around at all
And still a guilt awaits me
If I am ever to move on
From this place set below the hills
Will the headstone get lonely
And does it already from my
Lack of visitation
Promise me that if you need a friend
Like I do
Hitch a ride with the tree's breeze
And the butterflies
And we will brave this town and the others

Lack of Composure - January 5, 2022

They told me to put this pain
Into a song. And let its
melodies tell our story.
But after all these years,
I still feel like this loss
can't be set to a tune
Or lyrics to tell of the
Emptiness I still feel
When I'm reminded
That you're never coming back.
It's nauseating and bleak
And I don't think I could or would
Find what key this ache is in.

Errands - January 16, 2022

I'm driving and then it
hits me.
That store I hate
I never get to go with you again.
I'd run the most boring of errands
Just for the company.

Sour Plums - January 16, 2022

We don't see your friends much anymore
they were your friends, after all
But I wonder how they miss you
do they still watch the automatic doors
of their shop, and wait
for your entrance? catch a glimpse of
a dark mustache or tan bald spot
and wonder if the universe decided
to change its rules?

If I had to guess, memories of you
pop in like a plum just out of season
a tartness that makes you sigh
eye twitches, things are not as they should be
not as you wish them to be
but the bite is familiar and it takes you back
to not too long ago
when things were sweet and you didn't know how good you
had it.

Sprinter - January 16, 2022

You ran away so fast,
all the bridges you crossed burned
I don't think you even stopped to turn around
or if you did, you were so accustomed to the smell of smoke
and the grayness of ash, you couldn't see what you'd done

Even after you left me in rubble, you told me
"I'll always be in your corner, friend I deeply cherish"
and the only thing I'm left to do is wonder
how those words are defined so differently by the two of us

Outline of a Human - January 23, 2022

When did I become terrified
to exist as a whole person
So opposed to expose my full existence
with interests and obsessions
I've spent so long believing that to be defined
or rather confined
by my passions, it would be a tragedy

living in limbo
loving quietly
moving on quickly
hard to pin down

I convinced myself it was better to be impossible
to know, than stuck
unable to change
Limited by the image of me in others' heads

But I failed to realize that if I leave the blanks open
I love _____
I am _____
I crave _____
I hope _____
People will fill them in for me
And that is far worse than the risk of being allowed to
change or not

so today I am
shades of green
carnations over expensive flowers
pop music, oversized t-shirts, crossword puzzles
defined by all the things I love
and all the things I used to love
and all the things I cannot wait to love

Quick Morning Routine - May 15, 2022

Get ready for work
Moisturize and spf
Brush teeth, brush brows
Take the breath
That sighs out 8 years
Of compounded grief
Remember your death
Clutch the coin
Hung around my neck
One like yours
Of Turkish currency
My thumb brushes the ridged edge
In case genies have taken
New residence

Oops - June 4, 2022

Christmas party
Two thousand eighteen
Things were meant to be so breezy
Suddenly I was falling
Things were supposed to stay casual
Now you're opening up the door
With a key that looks just like the one on my ring
Don't know if stars aligned
Don't know about things meant to be
But I'm so happy things turned out differently

Notes to my Future Self - June 5, 2022

Do the little things.

Make the effort.

When you have a bit of energy

When you have the mental space

When there is a quiet rhythm and repetition

Step out and find a new act of love

Make a habit of newness

A pattern of different kindnesses.

Set plans to look forward to.

Keep dreaming, even simple dreams.

Forecast - September 22, 2022

I do not plan to be any one place
for very long
except lost
and in love with you

In Focus - September 24, 2022

You have stayed in color
While our friends turn sepia toned
And your eyes track to mine with lightning speed
All others have slowed even imperceptibly
And you are so, so here with me

Sugar and Salt - October 23, 2022

Now every beautiful moment
is also the most painful
because you are not here to share it with
Wedding bells
Baby's first cry
A blended chord
None resound purely sweet

A Cancer's Lament - December 26, 2022

And on the way home,
blink vigorously away
the blurring wet of tears
As there will never be another day precisely like this
As we will age
As we ebb and flow

Wash over the immediate nostalgia of a moment just passed

Hello Old Friend - January 6, 2023

Maybe you will go to the bookstore today

And thumb through the not yet dusty pages of the kind
cheesy YA novel we used to laugh about

And wonder if I remember you

Of course I do.

I even miss you, on accident

I take trips from memory lane to your Instagram

to see how wrong and how right we were

When we used to play What Ifs about the future

And, again on accident, I wait for you to complete your
leave of absence from my life

to prove that you left because you needed to, not because of
me

Of course I remember you

I'm writing this poem about you, aren't I?

A Break - March 15, 2023

I have come to a point in my life where grief sometimes feels like a sweet relief. A comfort, so contradictory. For it means that my life has slowed enough to reflect. A moment has been fought for so that I have time and at least a little space to remember what was and what could be.

Finity - April 6, 2023

The last sip of a morning iced coffee
slips down my throat
Nothing sweet ever lasts
no matter how slowly I savor the caramel
oat milk creamer, and search for energy to make it through
the day at the bottom of the cup
Scrub my scalp with my knuckles
and peel back food containers with the side of my thumb
so I don't hasten the chipping of my nail polish
But specks of shimmery green paint and bare pinky nail
corners spell out
Nothing beautiful ever lasts
And so it goes
The second coffee of a day cannot be separated from its
shaking anxieties, and second coats of nail polish are a sorry,
lumpy attempt to recover the lost
Nothing is forever
But there are still new mornings with their own cup full of
cold brew and there are still fresh manicures
To dawn our hands in a brand new beauty
Trust

Generational Heartache - April 25, 2023

I do not think it is by coincidence that grief is most often described as heavy. That sinking in your chest when you consider your lost loved one runs miles deep. For death's inevitability, you hold the memory of someone. But within their memory was someone(s) they lost who also lost who also lost who also lost. And so within your heart is ancestral aching for those who went beyond. I carry my father who carried his parents who carried their parents, and on it goes. You carry your best friend who carried their hero who carried their brother, and still it goes. With no intention of insensitivity, dead weight.

Of course you are tired. Of course you feel you cannot get up.

Reruns - May 25, 2023

I am so worried that you are fading
into a childhood cartoon
Vague, nostalgic, memorable but indistinct
I do not want to hear a theme song and think
it sounds familiar but cannot recall the words
I am begging for reruns

Rainier - June 20, 2023

I've never liked cherries
except Rainier
a truth I always held dear
Yellow, but a twinge of pink
A bite of home,
juice to drink. Washington
an anchor til I steadied
Thank you nightlight,
now I've found the sun

Heaven's Gate

There may be a day
when I arrive at a house beyond the light
Where you have been waiting for us
The key for it, I threw away many years ago
Hands no longer willing to clutch with such a fervor, of
prayer and devotion
And of shame and authority

My hands were made to rest open,
while sadness and recollection
and unapologetic rage and joy and indifference
All pass in between my fingers
that have slowly unclenched over such a time

There may or may not be a day
when I arrive at a house beyond the light
But if you are there waiting for us
I choose to trust that you would open the door

I cannot spend this time in between
searching for a key
instead of myself

Afterword

I suppose this is time to connect the dots. There is a mystery innate to poetry. There is more space on the page to insert yourself and feel intimacy with the untold. But I think it would be a disservice to us all to end this without an explicit discussion of why this book exists.

On March 9, 2014, Amjad "Jimmy" Aldulaimi died of an aggressive cancer. He was an Iraqi immigrant, friend to all, and the loving patriarch of my family. I was 15 when this catastrophe changed everything about me, but life did this silly and awful thing of continuing. And I had to figure out how to keep up while refusing to let go of such a loving father and his memory.

Four years after such an earth-shattering loss, depression and anxiety raging, I started bringing pen to paper in earnest and found little pieces of my Dad waiting for me there. The fruit motif throughout this book came from him. If you have an Arab parent, I think that will make sense to you. I mean, my dad had his own hand signal for figs, if that tells you anything.

However, this book is not exclusively about parental loss, or loss in general. It is both figs and falling. Falling and flailing, as a late teen/early twenty-something. Falling in and out of love, both romantic and self. Falling out of friendship. Falling from faith. It is skydiving without checking for the parachute. It is tripping repeatedly. It is the embarrassment of standing back up. It is the pride of standing back up.

Acknowledgements

Thank you to anyone reading. Thank you for seeing me and maybe allowing yourself to be seen in return.

To my family, I won the lottery with all of you. Except it is something more rare and precious, our bond.

To my therapist, you have been one of my few constants. Your gentle wisdom defines the term "guiding light" for me.

To Ryan, your love and partnership is the gift of my life. I would not have found the courage to share this work without your steadiness.

And finally, thank you to my dad. Baba, your belief in me was abundant and vibrantly sincere in life, it remains palpable from the other side. We will carry each other for the rest of my days.

www.ingramcontent.com/pod-product-compliance
Lightning Source LLC
Chambersburg PA
CBHW030502130626
46549CB00007B/2829